Did It Take Creativity to Find Relativity, Albert Einstein?

Melvin and Gilda Berger
illustrated by Brandon Dorman

SCHOLASTIC 🔆 NONFICTION
an imprint of
▟SCHOLASTIC

Contents

Who was Albert Einstein? 5

When was Einstein born? 6

When did Albert start to speak? 8

What happened when Albert was five years old? 11

What else influenced his life? 12

When did Albert start school? 14

Why did Albert switch schools? 17

Where did Einstein finish high school? 18

When did Einstein graduate college? 20

What important event happened in 1905? 23

What is the most famous equation in the world? 24

What did Einstein discover about light? 26

Try it out!

    Experiment #1 28

    Experiment #2 29

How could scientists test Einstein's theory? 31

Did the theory of relativity make Einstein famous? 32

Was Einstein happy in Germany? 34

Did Einstein marry again? 37

What theory did Einstein start working on
in the 1920s? 38

What happened when Einstein
went back to Germany? 40

How did Einstein help end World War II? 43

How do we remember Einstein? 45

Einstein time line 46

Index 48

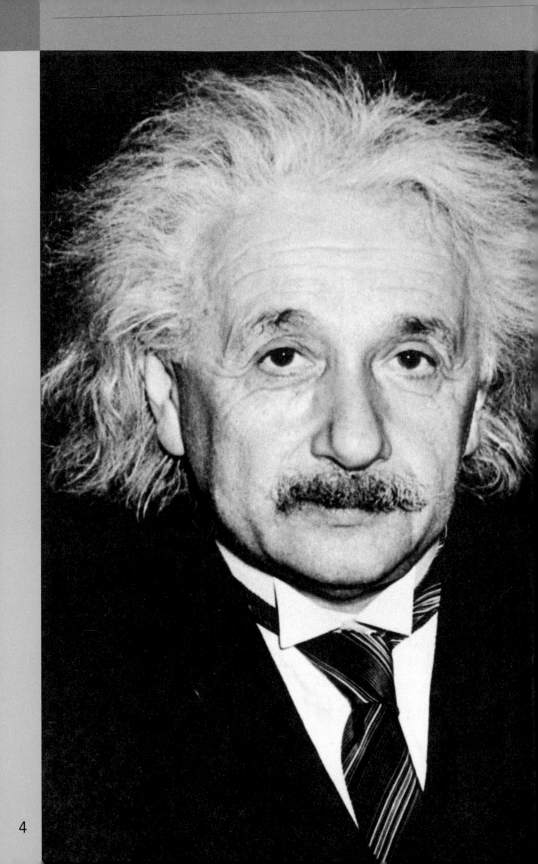

Who was Albert Einstein?

Many people call Albert Einstein the greatest scientist of all time. He is most famous for his theory of relativity.

Einstein discovered that when an object moves, it becomes shorter and heavier. He also realized that time flows more slowly for a moving object. But you can't notice these changes unless the object is moving thousands of miles a second! The theory that explains these effects is called the theory of relativity.

It takes many years of study to fully understand the theory of relativity. However, we can all grasp parts of the theory and get to know Einstein better.

Albert Einstein was a brilliant scientist whose theory of relativity changed our basic ideas of time, space, mass, and gravity.

When was Einstein born?

Albert Einstein was born on March 14, 1879, in the small town of Ulm, Germany. His father, Hermann Einstein, was a businessman. His mother, Pauline Koch Einstein, loved music and was a fine pianist. Both parents were Jewish and also proud Germans.

When Albert was one year old, his family moved to Munich,

Albert as a very young boy.

Father,
Hermann Einstein

Mother,
Pauline Koch Einstein

a much bigger German city. His sister, Maria, nicknamed Maja, was born there in 1881.

Albert's parents worried a great deal about their son. As an infant and a toddler, he looked odd. His head seemed too large for his body. He was also very shy and quiet. Most of the time he played by himself.

When did Albert start to speak?

Albert did not speak until he was about three years old. Some say that his first words were, "The soup is too hot." When asked why he had not spoken before, it is said that he replied, "Up to now everything has been fine."

One time, Albert's mother asked him to play with his sister, Maja. Albert thought she was some sort of toy. He asked, "Yes, but where are its wheels?"

Speech continued to be a problem while Albert was growing up. When asked a question, he often mumbled the words to himself a few times. Then he thought a while before giving an answer. His slow way of speaking made some people think that he was not very smart.

Albert with his younger sister, Maria, nicknamed Maja.

What happened when Albert was five years old?

His father gave Albert a compass. The young boy found the compass amazing. No matter how he twisted or turned it, the needle always pointed north!

Albert asked his father why this was so. His father said that the earth is like a giant magnet. Its force is all around. We cannot see it or feel it, but it pulls the compass pointer to the north — along with every other magnet in the world.

The compass raised lots of questions for Albert: How did this "hidden" force reach the compass? Do other things have "hidden" forces behind them? Einstein spent the rest of his life trying to answer these, and similar, questions!

Even at age five, Albert was asking hard questions.

What else influenced his life?

When he was about six years old, Einstein's mother bought her son a violin. She also hired a music teacher to give him lessons.

At first, the boy was not too happy to have to practice every day. But soon he came to love the violin. He even began to enjoy practicing. The young Albert played duets with his mother. He would play the violin and she would accompany him on the piano.

Einstein's early love for music stayed with him for life. Making music, alone or with others, gave the great scientist many hours of pleasure and relaxation.

When did Albert start school?

At the age of six, Albert entered a Catholic elementary school. He did not enjoy it. The other boys teased him because he was the only Jewish child in his class. Some did not like him because he would not play sports. Also, his teachers thought he was rude because he asked too many questions.

At home, his parents gave Albert books to read. They urged him to ask questions. Eager to learn more, Albert taught himself advanced math. He also tried to understand the world better. For example, he wondered about light: What would it be like to travel on a beam of light? Can anything go faster than light?

Schoolboy Albert with Maja, who is holding a parasol.

Why did Albert switch schools?

When Albert was fifteen, his father moved the family to Milan, Italy, where he started a new business. Albert stayed in Munich to finish high school. The young man was lonely and unhappy. He did not like the way he was being taught. He had to memorize facts, repeat them back, and was not allowed to ask questions. While he got high marks in math and science, he did not do well in other subjects.

After only one term, Albert quit school to join his family in Italy. He also made two important decisions: He would give up his German citizenship, and he would finish high school in a different country.

Seventeen-year-old Einstein, seated at the left, with his high school class in Switzerland.

Where did Einstein finish high school?

Einstein finally graduated from high school in Switzerland, which was just across the border from his parents' home in Italy. After graduation, he applied to a college, the Swiss Federal Polytechnic Institute. He failed the first entrance exam. But he tried again the next year — and he passed.

In college, Albert studied math and science. He lived in a small, dark room. Since he had very little money for food, he often went hungry.

But now Albert made new friends. One was Mileva Maric, the only woman in his class. He liked her very much. They would spend hours together, talking about their studies.

Einstein, Mileva Maric, and their college friends often gathered together to study and talk.

When did Einstein graduate college?

Einstein graduated from college in 1900. However, the next two years were hard. He wanted to teach science in a college, but could not find a job. He wanted to marry Mileva, but had no money to support a family.

In 1902, he got lucky. He found a job in the Swiss patent office. It was where people sent ideas for new inventions. Albert had to make sure that the inventions really worked. It wasn't the job he wanted, but it gave him an income and free time to work on his own science projects. Albert married Mileva in 1903. The next year, their first son, Hans Albert, was born.

This 1904 photograph shows Einstein, his first wife, Mileva, and their son, Hans Albert.

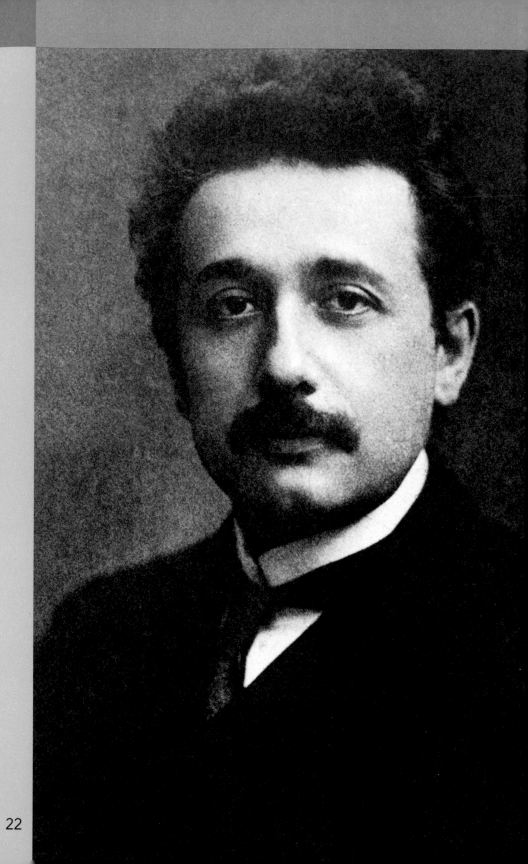

What important event happened in 1905?

While working at the patent office, Einstein wrote what he called his special theory of relativity. Relativity is a way of looking at something compared with something else. Einstein worked out his theory of relativity with all kinds of "thought experiments."

Here's a thought experiment to help you understand relativity: Imagine you are standing at a train station and see a train speed by. Compared with you, or relative to you, the train is going very fast. Now, imagine you are in a car moving in the same direction and at the same speed as the train. Relative to you, the train is standing still. That's relativity!

Einstein was only twenty-six years old when he wrote his monumental special theory of relativity.

What is the most famous equation in the world?

Almost everyone agrees it is Einstein's equation, $E=mc^2$. "E" is energy, which can occur as heat, light, or sound; "m" is mass, the amount of matter or stuff in something; "c" stands for the speed of light — 186,000 miles per second (300,000 kps). When "c" is multiplied by itself as "c^2," it is a huge number. It tells us that just a little mass can be changed into a FANTASTIC amount of energy.

$E=mc^2$ is a most amazing equation. With this knowledge, scientists are able to produce huge amounts of energy from tiny bits of mass. The heat energy that comes from changing mass into energy is called nuclear energy. Nuclear energy now drives many submarines, runs power plants that supply electricity to vast areas, and has a number of medical uses.

HRE RELATIVITÄT – ATOME – QUANTEN

55

$$E = mc^2$$

DEUTSCHLAND

A. Einstein

200

In 2005, Germany issued a postage stamp honoring Einstein and his theory.

What did Einstein discover about light?

Before Einstein, scientists were not sure whether light always travels in a straight line or whether gravity curves its path. Einstein discovered that the pull of gravity *does* bend light. He also discovered a way to measure how much the light is bent. He published this idea in 1916, in addition to his special theory of relativity. He called it the general theory of relativity.

Einstein said that the strong pull of the gravity of stars and planets can bend light.

He explained that the gravity doesn't reach out and grab the light. Rather, the gravity curves the shape of space, adding hills and valleys. As light passes through the curved space, it bends.

Light from distant stars is bent as it passes through space.

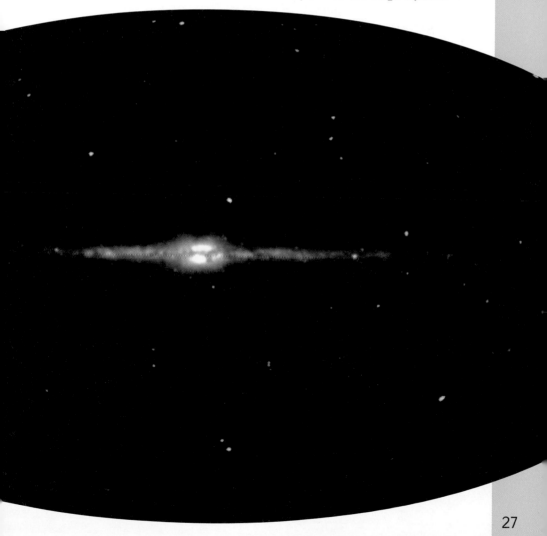

Try it out!
Experiment #1: "See" light bend.

Picture yourself inside a glass rocket. It is shooting upward at a high speed, faster and faster. Someone in space shines a flashlight at the rocket. Inside, you see the beam of light enter through one wall. It crosses the rocket and leaves through the opposite wall. The rocket is going up, so the light exits at a lower point through the opposite wall.

0:06

0:0

As it crosses the rocket, the light would appear to move in a curved line. The faster the acceleration of the rocket, the more curved the path.

Try it out!

Experiment #2: "See" light bend.

Picture a trampoline. Roll a baseball across the top. The baseball rolls straight across.

Now picture a trampoline with a big bowling ball weighing down the middle. When you roll the baseball again, it swoops down toward the dent, or curve, made by the bowling ball.

The path of the baseball bends because the bowling ball changes the shape of the trampoline. In the same way, a beam of light bends when gravity changes the shape of space. And that's why we can see light bend!

Earth

Moon

Sun

Real
location
of Hyade
in the sk

"Wrong" location of
Hyades in the sky

How could scientists test Einstein's theory?

Scientists could prove Einstein was right if they could see the light from distant stars bend as it passes near the sun. Since they knew the exact place of the Hyades stars in the sky, they decided to photograph them just before they passed behind the sun. If Einstein was right, the sun's gravity would bend the stars' light. The stars would seem to be in a different, or "wrong," place.

The sun's bright light hides the light coming from other stars. So scientists had to wait until the solar eclipse on May 29, 1919, when the moon blocked all of the sun's light. Photos did show the Hyades in the "wrong" place. Einstein was proved right! His figures showed exactly how much the sun's gravity had bent the light.

Above: A solar eclipse.
Below: This diagram shows how light bends.

Did the theory of relativity make Einstein famous?

Even before he was proved right, Einstein became world famous. He got a job as a professor of physics in Switzerland. Students loved his simple way of explaining difficult ideas. He lectured and visited universities all over Europe.

In 1913, Einstein was offered a university job in Berlin, Germany. His only duty was to think about his ideas. But there was one big problem. His wife, Mileva, did not want to leave Switzerland. She stayed there with their second son, Eduard, and Hans Albert.

Einstein moved to Berlin alone. After a while, Mileva and Albert were divorced.

Einstein did a great deal of reading — and writing — in the field of physics.

Was Einstein happy in Germany?

No, Einstein was very unhappy. World War I began in 1914. Germany fought several countries in Europe. In 1917, the United States entered the war against Germany.

Einstein hated all war. At the university, Einstein was attacked for his views against war and for being a Jew.

Einstein spoke out bravely. He became interested in finding a homeland for the Jewish people. (The state of Israel had not yet been founded.) It was a movement called Zionism. Many thought that Einstein would end up in jail, but he managed to stay free. In 1918, Germany lost the war.

American soldiers head to France in 1917.

In April 1917, the United States joined the war against Germany.

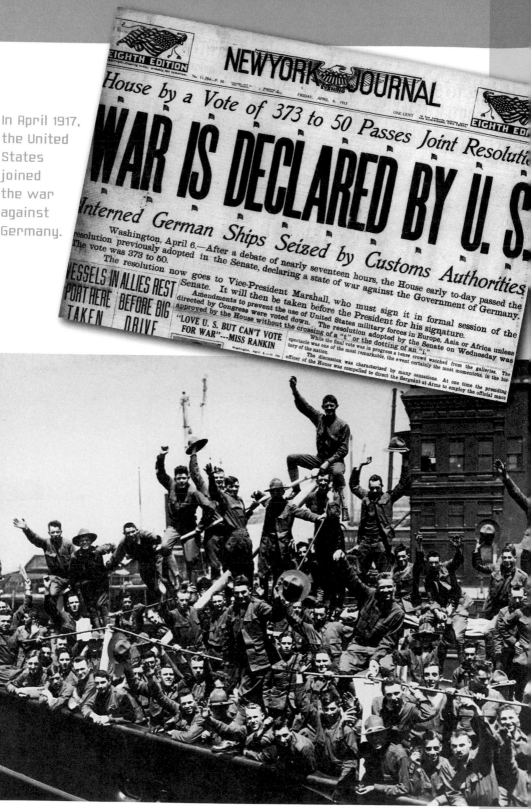

NEW YORK EVENING JOURNAL

FRIDAY, APRIL 6, 1917   ONE CENT

No. 11,784—P. M.

House by a Vote of 373 to 50 Passes Joint Resolution

WAR IS DECLARED BY U. S.

Interned German Ships Seized by Customs Authorities

Washington, April 6.—After a debate of nearly seventeen hours, the House early to-day passed the resolution previously adopted in the Senate, declaring a state of war against the Government of Germany. The vote was 373 to 50.

The resolution now goes to Vice-President Marshall, who must sign it in formal session of the Senate. It will then be taken before the President for his signature. The resolution adopted by the Senate on Wednesday was directed by Congress were voted down. Amendments to prevent the use of United States military forces in Europe, Asia or Africa unless approved by the House without the crossing of a "t" or the dotting of an "i."

While the final vote was in progress a tense crowd watched from the galleries. The spectacle was one of the most remarkable, the event certainly the most momentous, in the history of the nation.

The discussion was characterized by many sensations. At one time the presiding officer of the House was compelled to direct the Sergeant-at-Arms to employ the official mace

VESSELS IN | ALLIES REST
PORT HERE | BEFORE BIG
TAKEN | DRIVE

"LOVE U. S. BUT CAN'T VOTE FOR WAR"---MISS RANKIN

Washington, April 6.—In the

Einstein with his second wife, Elsa.

Did Einstein marry again?

In 1919, Einstein married his cousin, Elsa, in Germany. Elsa did her best to take good care of Albert. But he still often wore wrinkled clothes that did not fit. When he refused to wear socks, he said, "I am old enough to do what I want to do." Since he rarely had haircuts, his hair always looked wild.

In 1921, Einstein traveled to the United States. His purpose was to raise money for a Jewish homeland. When he arrived in New York, thousands of people were on hand to greet him. There was a huge parade. The president invited him to the White House. That year he won the Nobel Prize for physics.

What theory did Einstein work on starting in the 1920s?

Einstein began to work on his unified theory. The main idea is that there is a single, master theory that joins together many separate theories on how the universe works. Einstein tested many complicated equations, trying to find the one that would explain everything from what holds atoms together to what keeps huge planets and stars moving through space.

From the late 1920s until the end of his life, Einstein searched for the unified theory. He said he would have been happy just to learn that there was no such theory. But he never succeeded. Work on this theory continues today.

Einstein's lectures attracted large crowds of
scientists and students.

What happened when Einstein went back to Germany?

After his United States visit, Einstein found life worse than ever in Germany. Adolf Hitler and his Nazi Party were taking over the country. They jailed and killed Jews and people they called "enemies of the state." The Nazis burned books, including those written by Einstein. Einstein felt that his life was in danger.

Albert and Elsa fled Germany. They traveled to many countries, including the United States.

In the 1930s, Hitler and the Nazis in Germany burned books and passed harsh laws against German Jews.

In October 1933, they decided to settle in America. Einstein took a job at the Institute for Advanced Study in Princeton, New Jersey. Here, leading scientists and scholars were invited to do their own research.

Albert Einstein
Old Grove Rd.
Nassau Point
Peconic, Long Island

August 2nd, 1939

F.D. Roosevelt,
President of the United States,
White House
Washington, D.C.

Sir:

Some recent work by E.Fermi and L. Szilard, which has been com-
municated to me in manuscript, leads me to expect that the element uranium may be turned into a new and important source of energy in the immediate future. Certain aspects of the situation which has arisen seem
to call for watchfulness and, if necessary, quick action on the part
of the Administration. I believe therefore that it is my duty to bring
to your attention the following facts and recommendations:

In the course of the last four months it has been made probable -
through the work of Joliot in France as well as Fermi and Szilard in
America - that it may become possible to set up a nuclear chain reaction
in a large mass of uranium,by which vast amounts of power and large quant-
ities of new radium-like elements would be generated. Now it appears
almost certain that this could be achieved in the immediate future.

This new phenomenon would also lead to the construction of bombs,
and it is conceivable - though much less certain - that extremely power-
ful bombs of a new type may thus be constructed. A single bomb of this
type, carried by boat and exploded in a port, might very well destroy
the whole port together with some of the surrounding territory. However,
such bombs might very well prove to be too heavy for transportation by
air.

of uranium in moderate
the former Czechoslovaki
gian Congo.

desirable to have some
ration and the group
ca. One possible way
this task a person
in an inofficial

hem informed of the
for Government action
ng a supply of uran-

work,which is at present being car-
within the limits of the budgets of University laboratories, by
providing funds, if such funds be required, through his contacts with
private persons who are willing to make contributions for this cause,
and perhaps also by obtaining the co-operation of industrial laboratories
which have the necessary equipment.

I understand that Germany has actually stopped the sale of uranium
from the Czechoslovakian mines which she has taken over. That she should
have taken such early action might perhaps be understood on the ground
that the son of the German Under-Secretary of State, von Weizsäcker, is
attached to the Kaiser-Wilhelm-Institut in Berlin where some of the
American work on uranium is now being repeated.

Yours very truly,

A. Einstein

(Albert Einstein)

How did Einstein help end World War II?

World War II, which started in 1939, was between the Axis Powers (Germany, Japan, and Italy) and the Allies (United States, Britain, France, China, and Russia). Einstein knew that German scientists were trying to make an atomic bomb. Afraid that they might succeed, Einstein urged President Franklin D. Roosevelt to launch an effort in the United States to make one first. The United States became the first country to build and use an atomic bomb. Within a month, the war was over.

Throughout times of war and peace, Einstein continued to play the violin and go sailing. On April 18, 1955, at age seventy-six, Einstein died in Princeton, New Jersey.

How do we remember Einstein?

We remember Einstein as one of the most outstanding thinkers of all time. He was the first to realize that space, time, and length are all relative. They do not always stay the same.

We also remember Einstein because he used his fame to help people. He worked hard for peace, justice, and freedom.

Einstein stated the theory of relativity and made many other scientific discoveries. But that doesn't mean that he never made any mistakes. Einstein said, "Anyone who has never made a mistake has never tried anything new." We should all remember that!

Einstein at work in his study at Princeton. This brilliant, serious scientist enjoyed going without socks and fooling around when he could.

Einstein time line

1879	Albert Einstein is born in Ulm, Germany
1880	Family moves to Munich, Germany
1881	Sister, Maria, is born
1884	Father gives him a compass
1885	Starts school; starts playing the violin
1894	Family moves to Italy without Albert; Albert leaves high school
1896	Starts college at Swiss Federal Polytechnic Institute
1900	Graduates from college
1901	Becomes a Swiss citizen
1902	Gets job in Swiss patent office
1903	Marries Mileva Maric
1904	Son, Hans Albert, is born